ANIMAL SAFARI

Cheetahs

by Megan Borgert-Spaniol

BELLWETHER MEDIA • MINNEAPOLIS, MN

Note to Librarians, Teachers, and Parents:

Blastoff! Readers are carefully developed by literacy experts and combine standards-based content with developmentally appropriate text.

Level 1 provides the most support through repetition of high-frequency words, light text, predictable sentence patterns, and strong visual support.

Level 2 offers early readers a bit more challenge through varied simple sentences, increased text load, and less repetition of high-frequency words.

Level 3 advances early-fluent readers toward fluency through increased text and concept load, less reliance on visuals, longer sentences, and more literary language.

Level 4 builds reading stamina by providing more text per page, increased use of punctuation, greater variation in sentence patterns, and increasingly challenging vocabulary.

Level 5 encourages children to move from "learning to read" to "reading to learn" by providing even more text, varied writing styles, and less familiar topics.

Whichever book is right for your reader, Blastoff! Readers are the perfect books to build confidence and encourage a love of reading that will last a lifetime!

This edition first published in 2012 by Bellwether Media, Inc.

No part of this publication may be reproduced in whole or in part without written permission of the publisher. For information regarding permission, write to Bellwether Media, Inc., Attention: Permissions Department, 5357 Penn Avenue South, Minneapolis, MN 55419.

Library of Congress Cataloging-in-Publication Data

Borgert-Spaniol, Megan, 1989-
  Cheetahs / by Megan Borgert-Spaniol.
    p. cm. – (Blastoff! readers. Animal safari)
  Includes bibliographical references and index.
  Summary: "Developed by literacy experts for students in kindergarten through grade three, this book introduces cheetahs to young readers through leveled text and related photos"–Provided by publisher.
  ISBN 978-1-60014-716-6 (hardcover : alk. paper)
  1. Cheetah–Juvenile literature. I. Title.
  QL737.C23B667 2012
  599.75'9–dc23   2011028870

Printed in the United States of America, North Mankato, MN.

010112   1207

Contents

What Are Cheetahs?

Cheetahs are the fastest land **mammals** in the world.

Their sharp **claws** grip the ground when they run. Their long tails help them **balance** and turn.

Cheetahs live and hunt on grasslands. They **stalk** hares, antelopes, and other **prey**.

Cheetahs hide in tall grass as they move toward prey. Then they attack!

A cheetah takes its kill to a safe spot. It eats before lions or hyenas show up.

The cheetah cannot protect its food from these other **predators**. It can only run away.

Cubs

A female cheetah has 3 to 5 **cubs**. She carries them around in her mouth.

Cubs stay with their mother for one or two years. She teaches them how to hunt.

A mother catches live prey for her cubs to hunt. Your turn, cubs!

Glossary

balance—to stay steady and not fall

claws—sharp, curved nails at the end of an animal's fingers and toes

cubs—young cheetahs

mammals—warm-blooded animals that have backbones and feed their young milk

predators—animals that hunt other animals for food

prey—animals that are hunted by other animals for food

stalk—to secretly follow; cheetahs stalk their prey.

To Learn More

AT THE LIBRARY

Clarke, Ginjer L. *Cheetah Cubs*. New York, N.Y.: Grosset & Dunlap, 2007.

Squire, Ann O. *Cheetahs*. New York, N.Y.: Children's Press, 2005.

Wells, Robert E. *What's Faster Than a Speeding Cheetah?* Morton Grove, Ill.: A. Whitman, 1997.

ON THE WEB

Learning more about cheetahs is as easy as 1, 2, 3.

1. Go to www.factsurfer.com.

2. Enter "cheetahs" into the search box.

3. Click the "Surf" button and you will see a list of related Web sites.

With factsurfer.com, finding more information is just a click away.

Index